This

COLORING BOOK

BELONGS TO

____

____

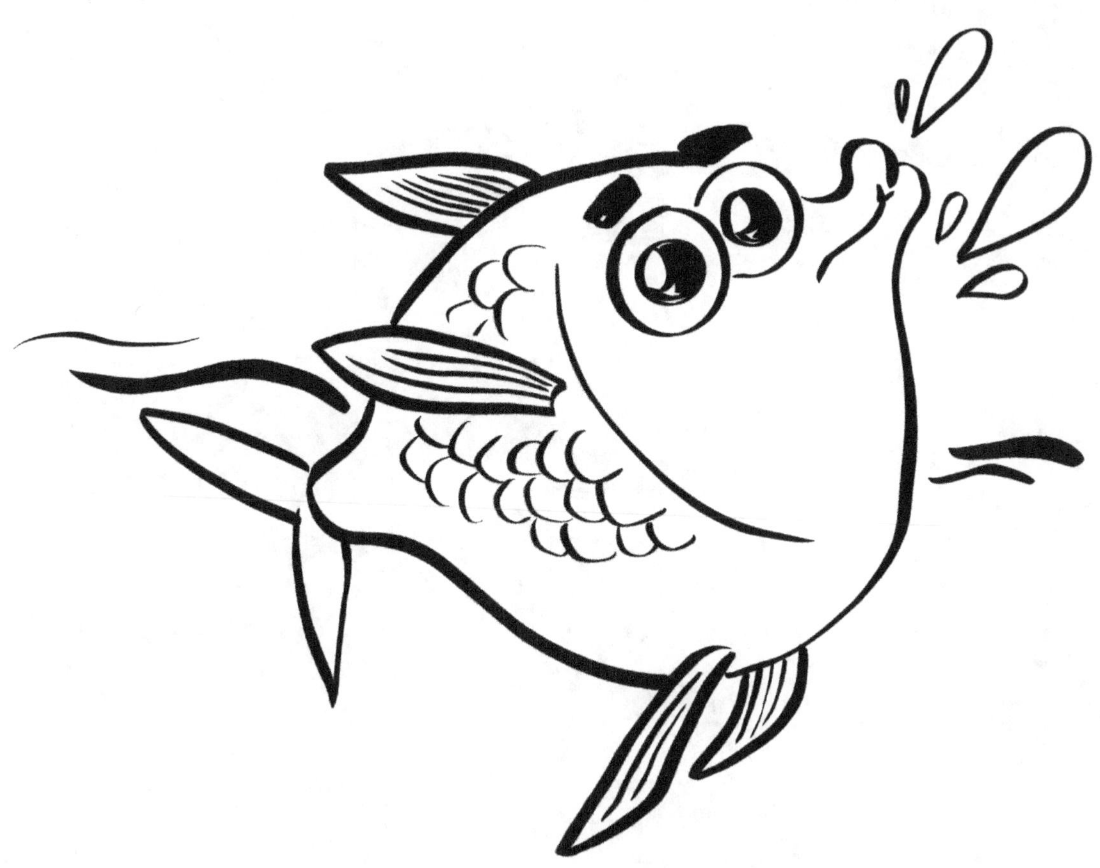

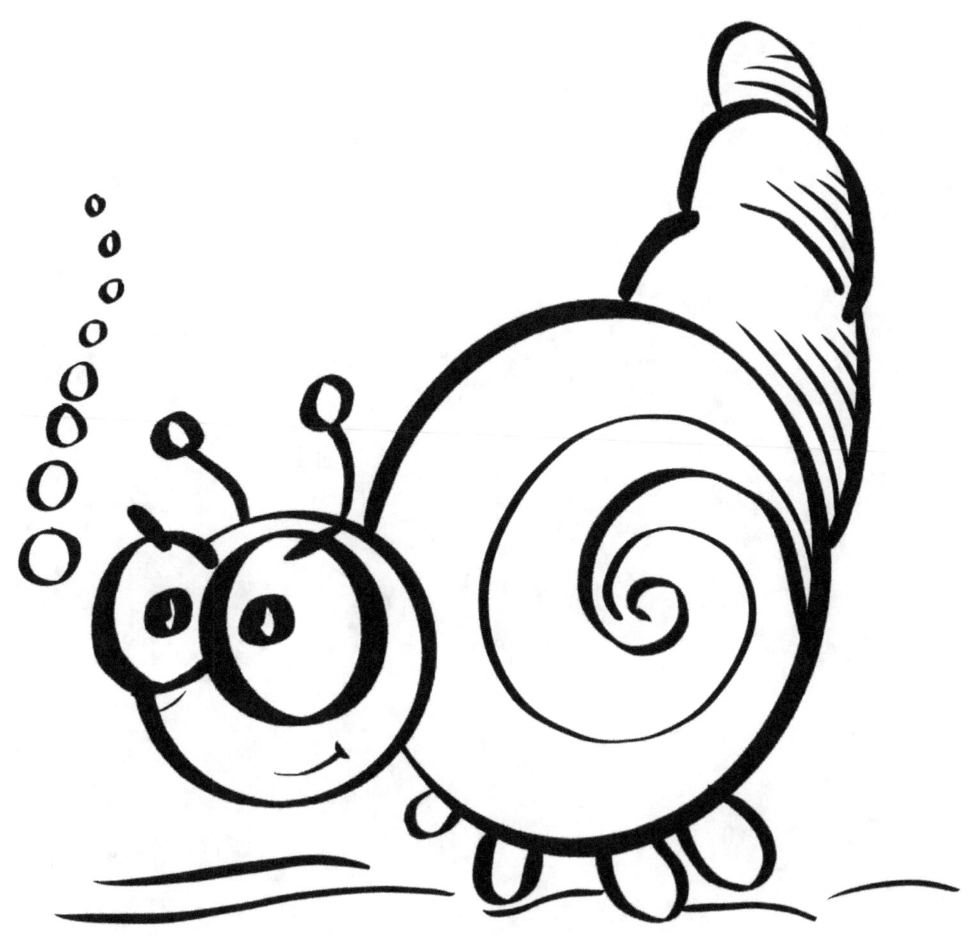

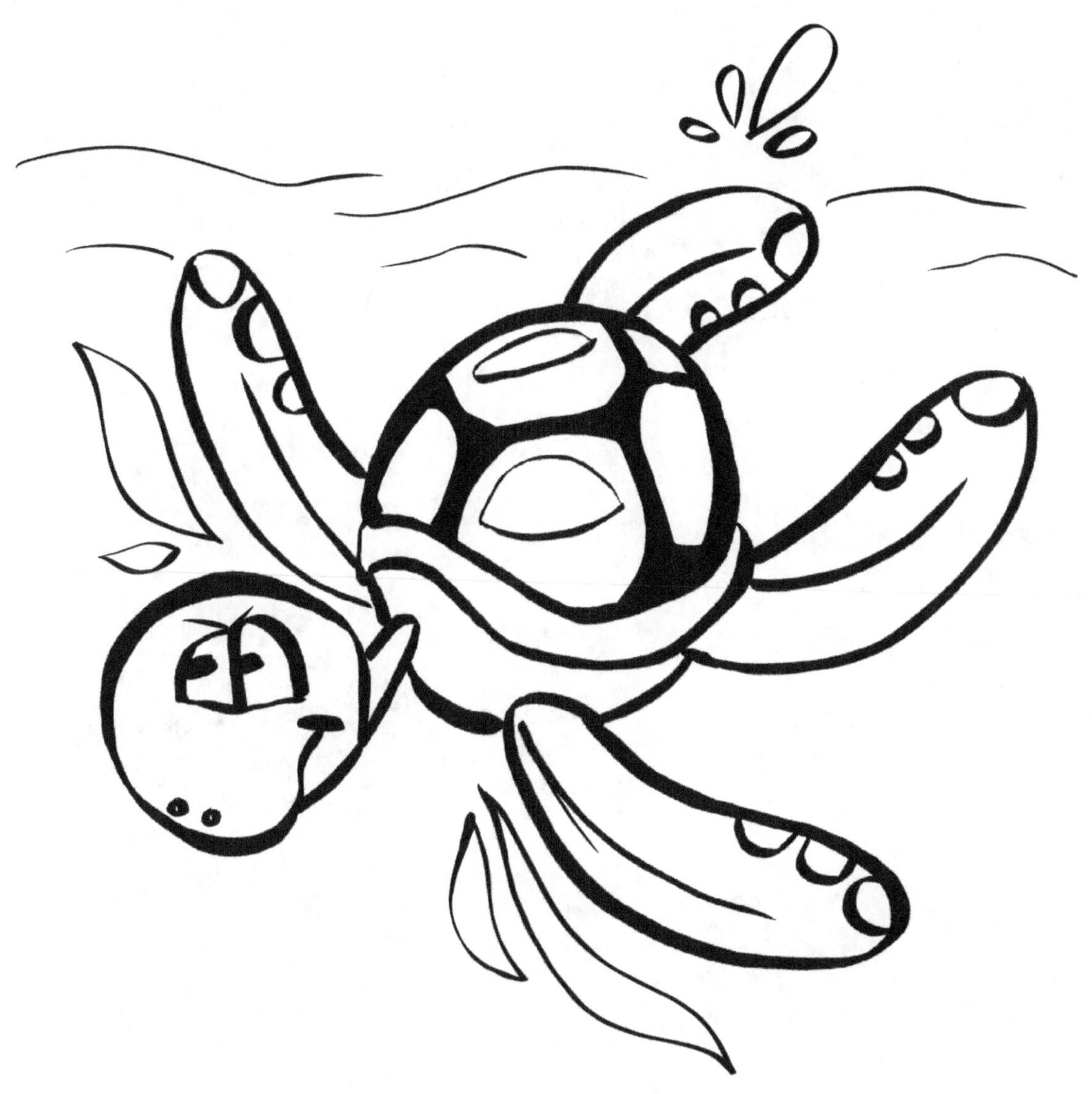

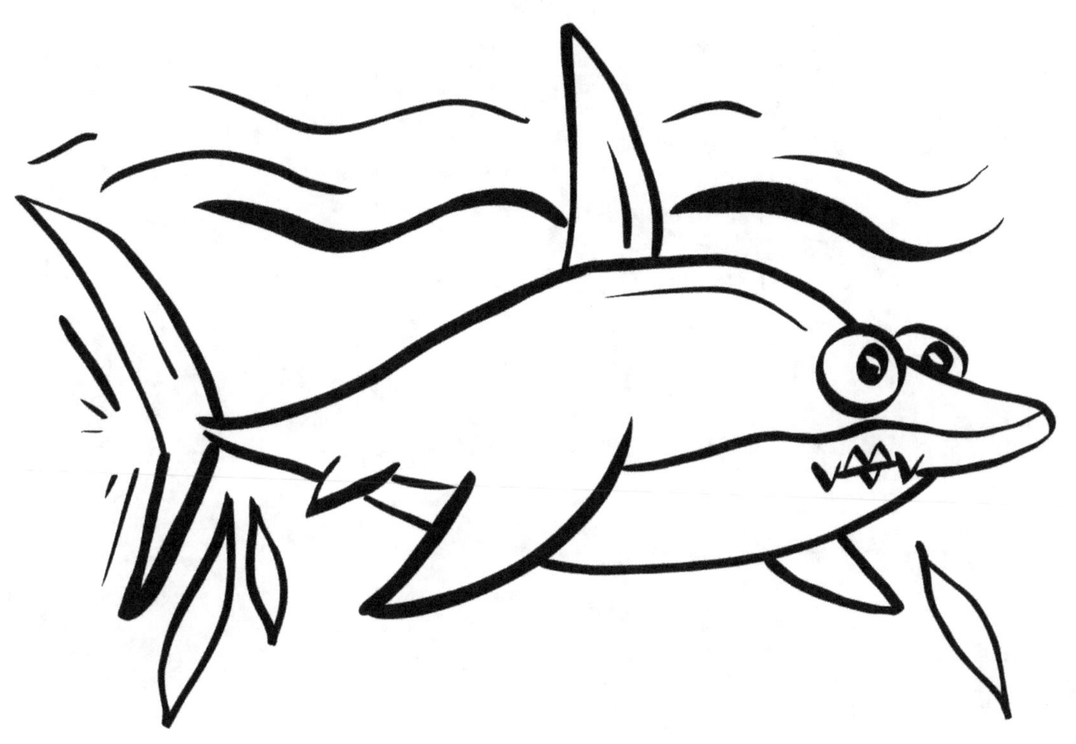

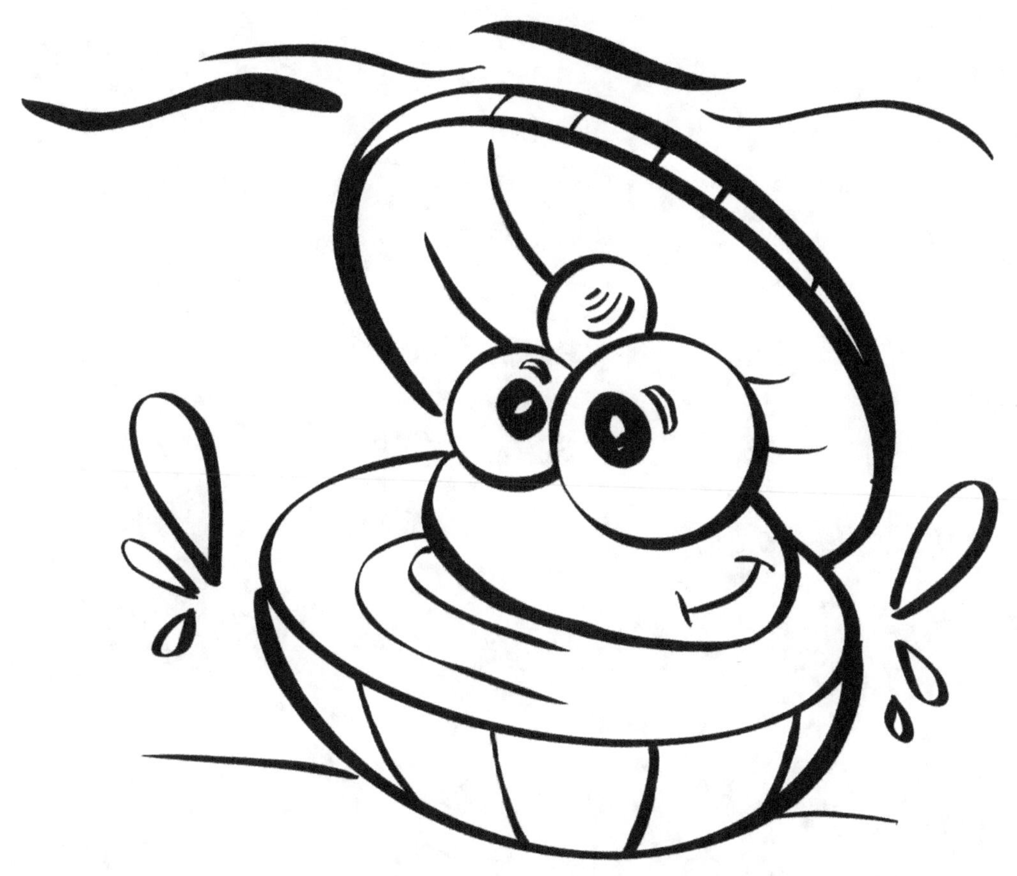

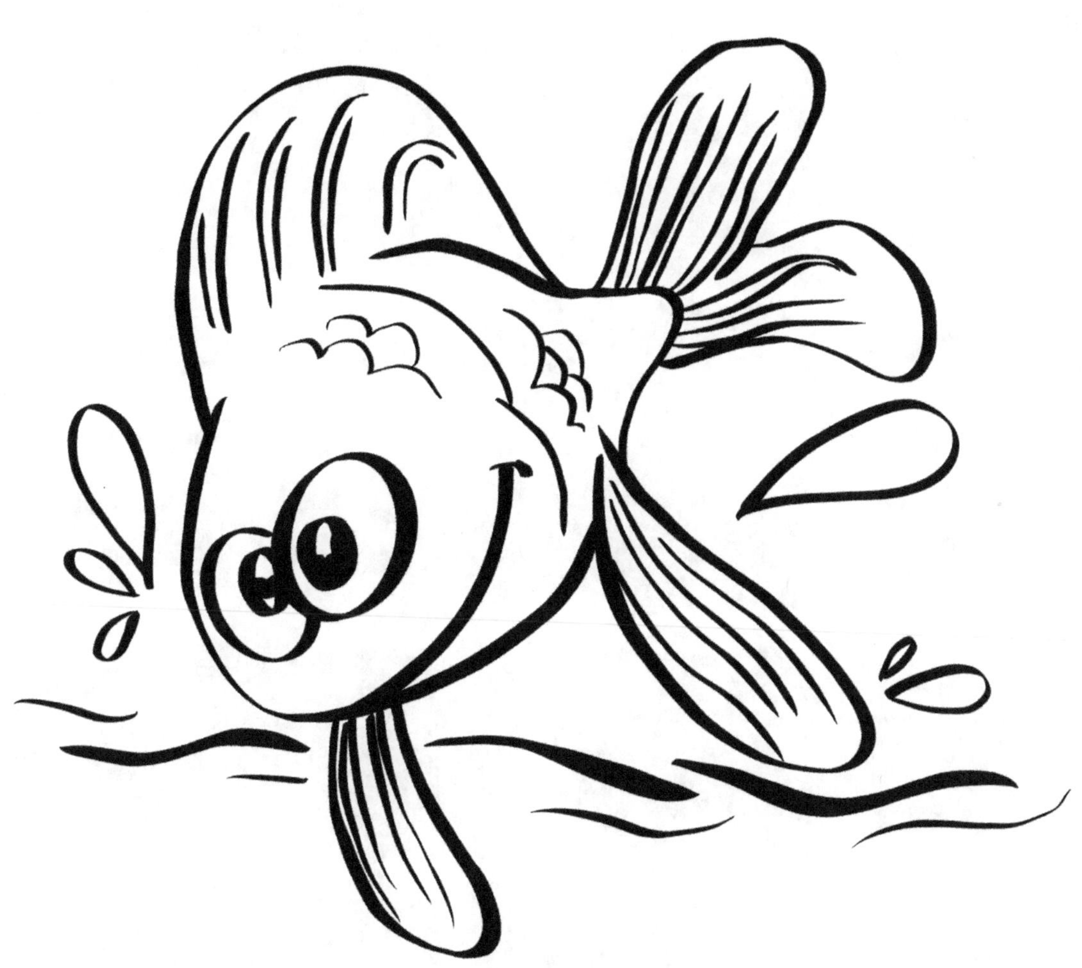

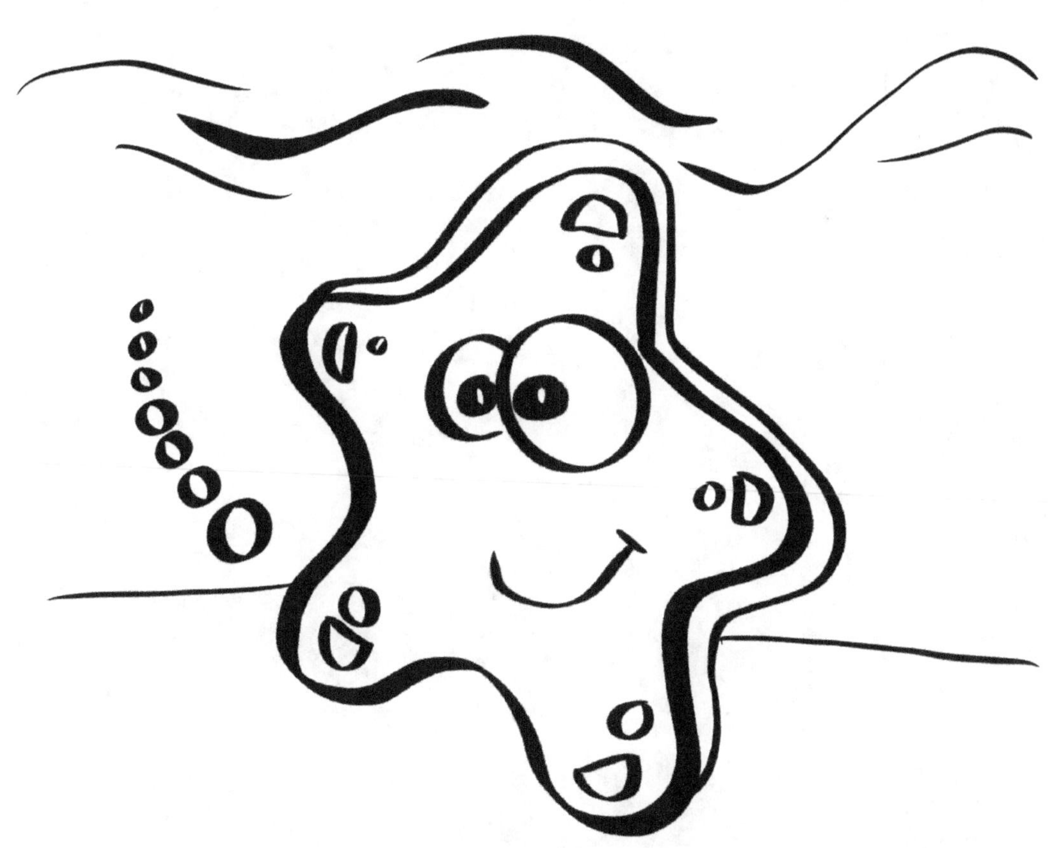

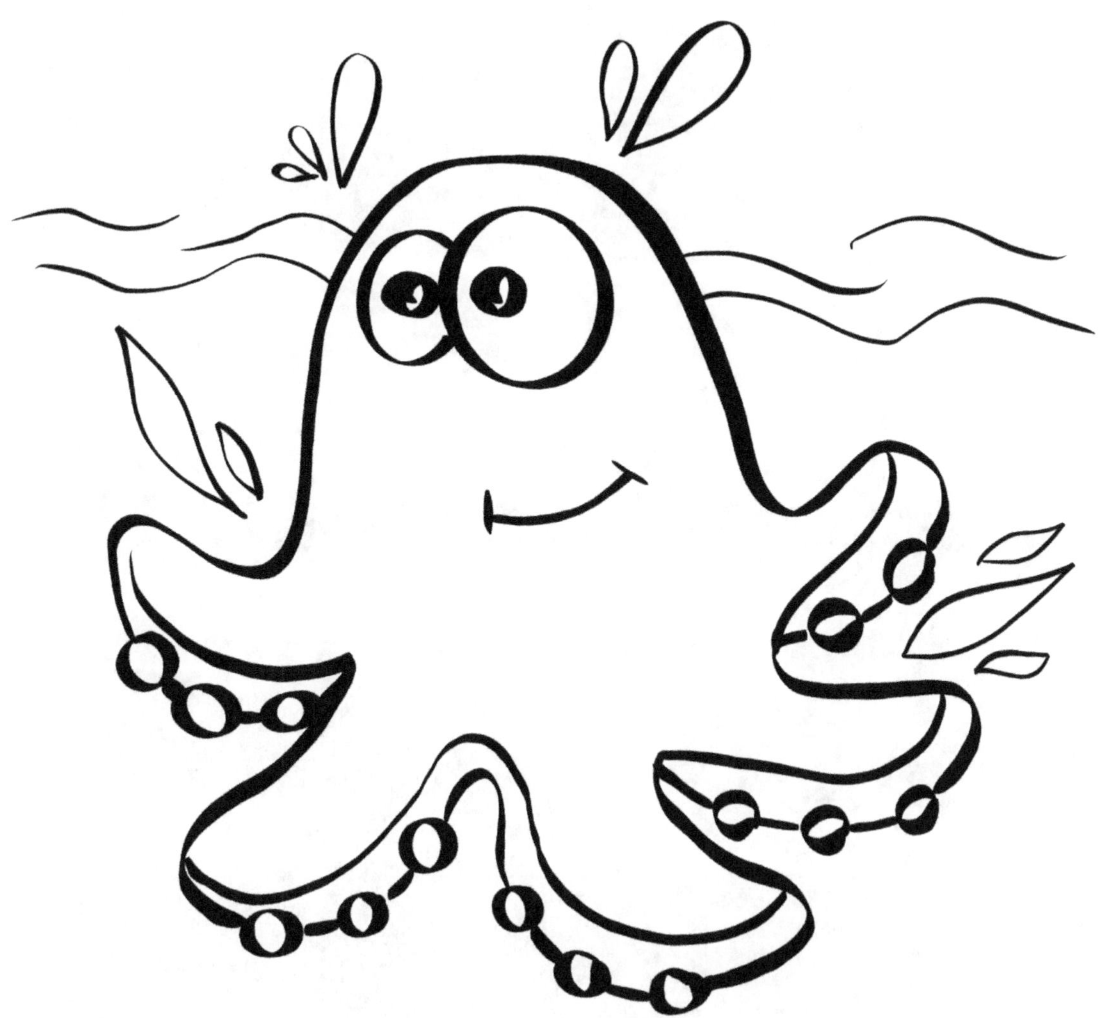

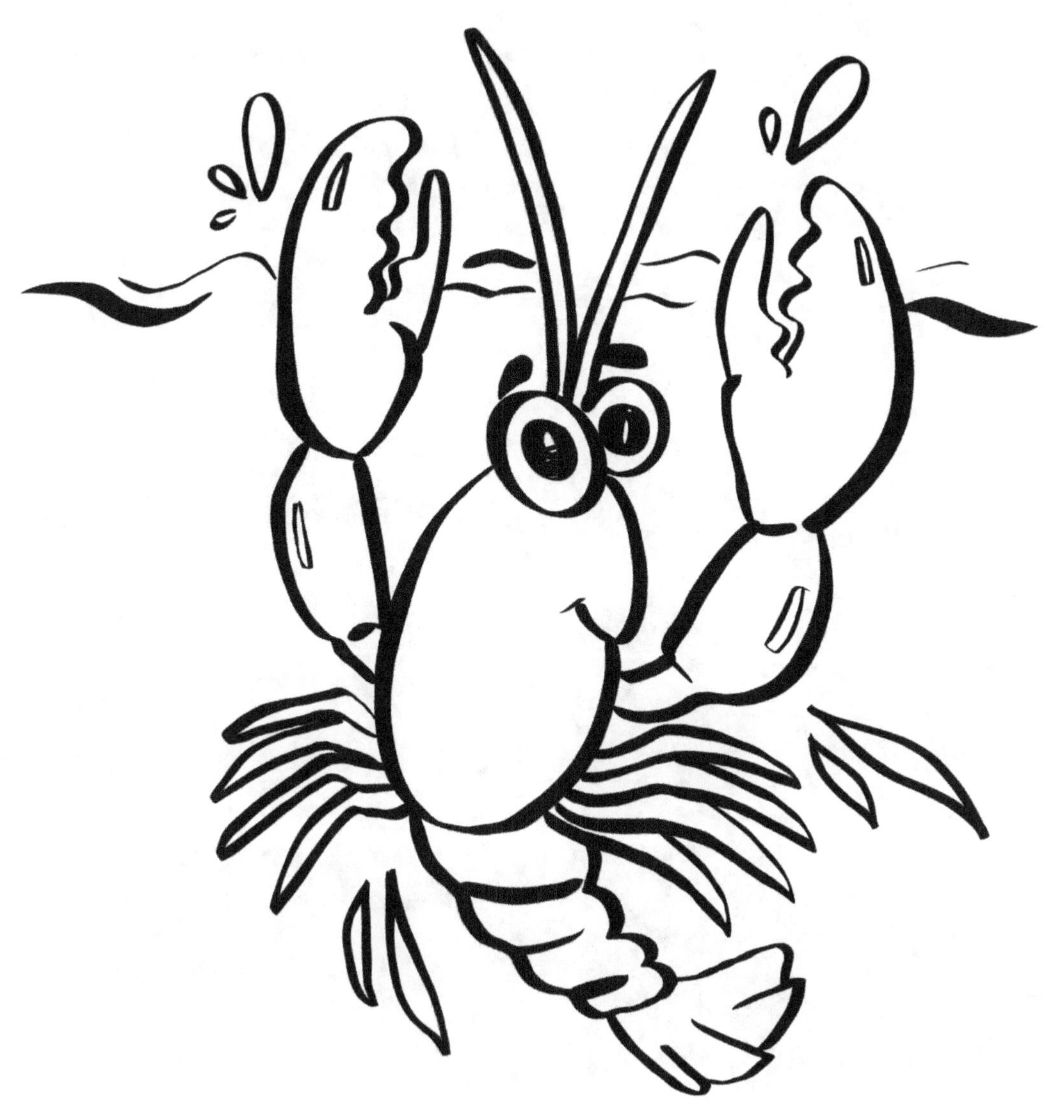

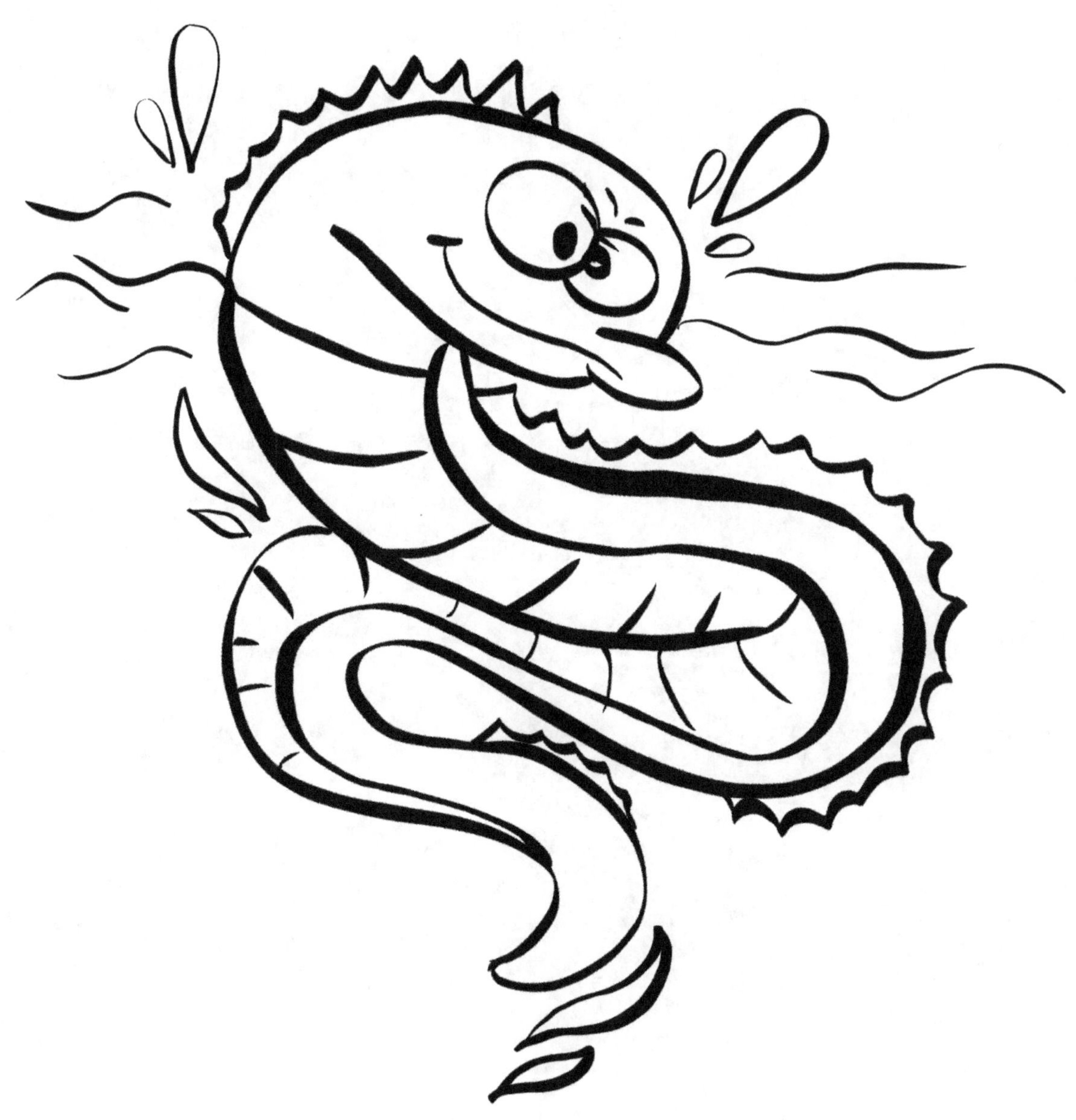

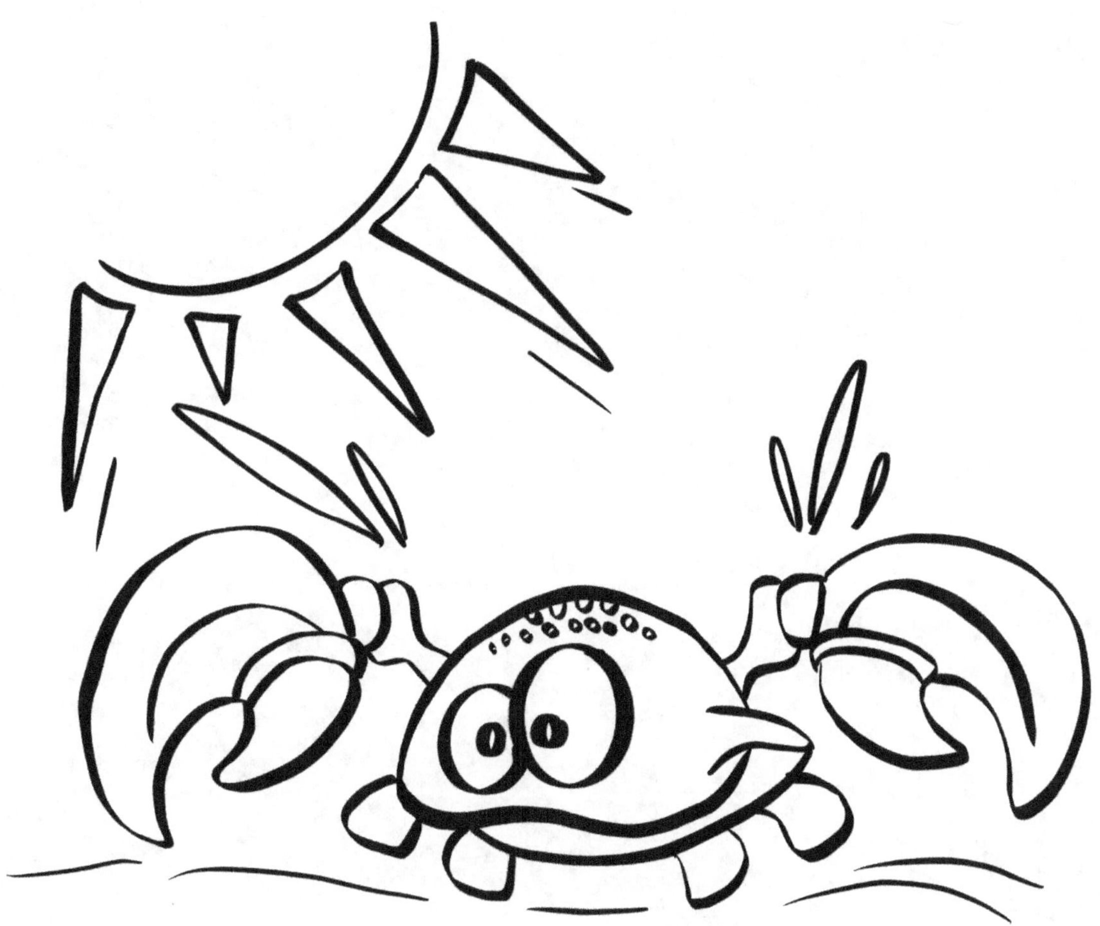

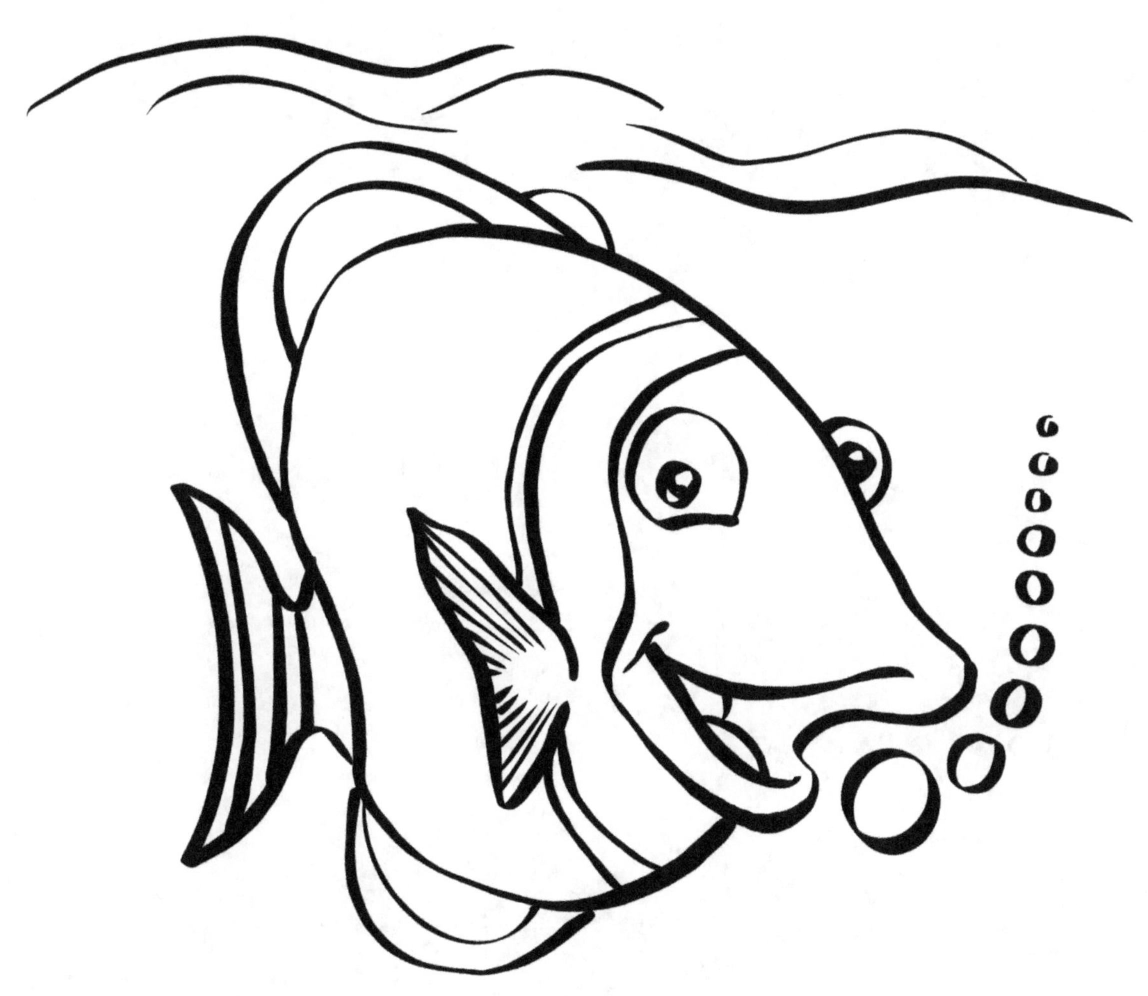

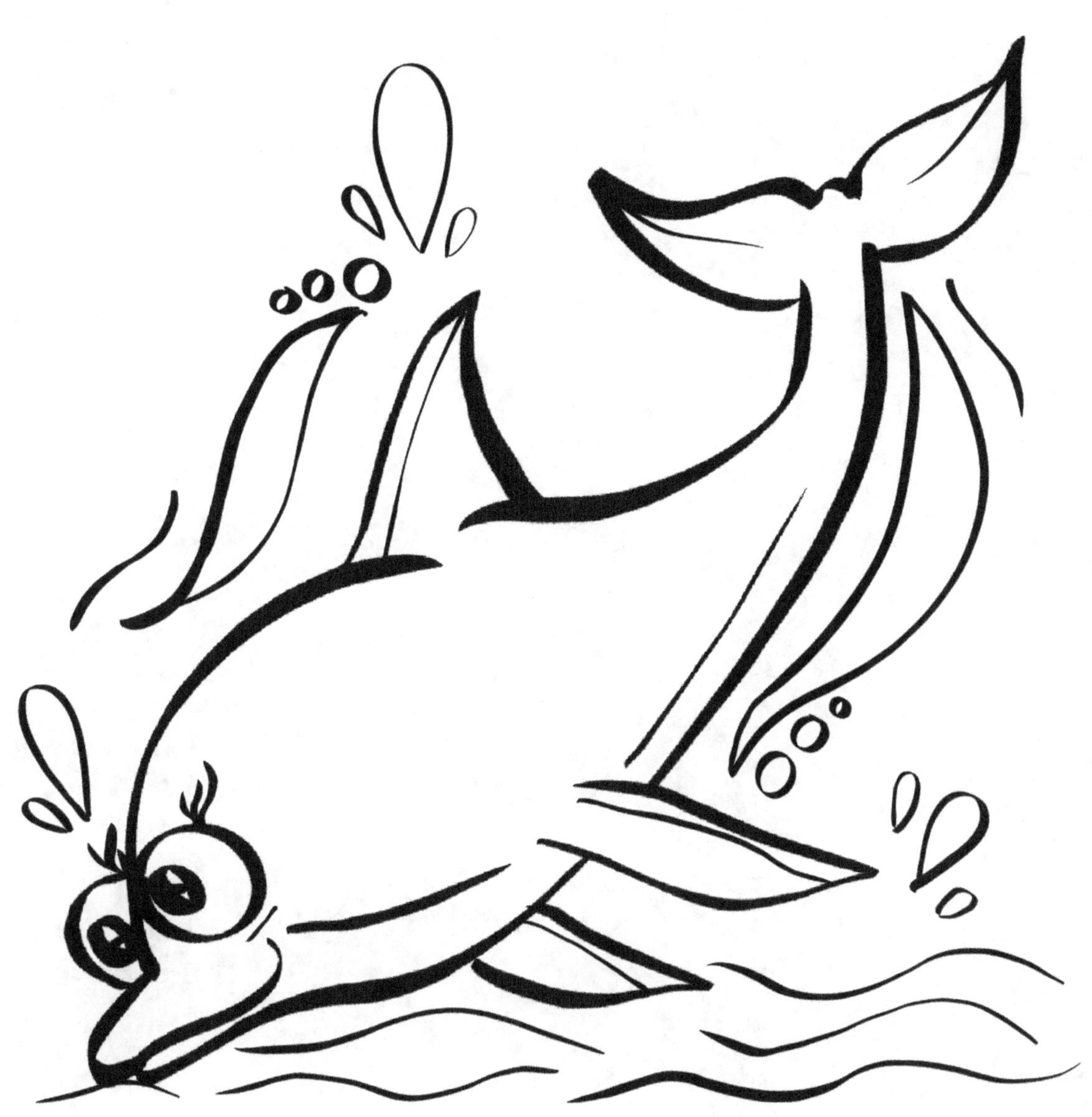

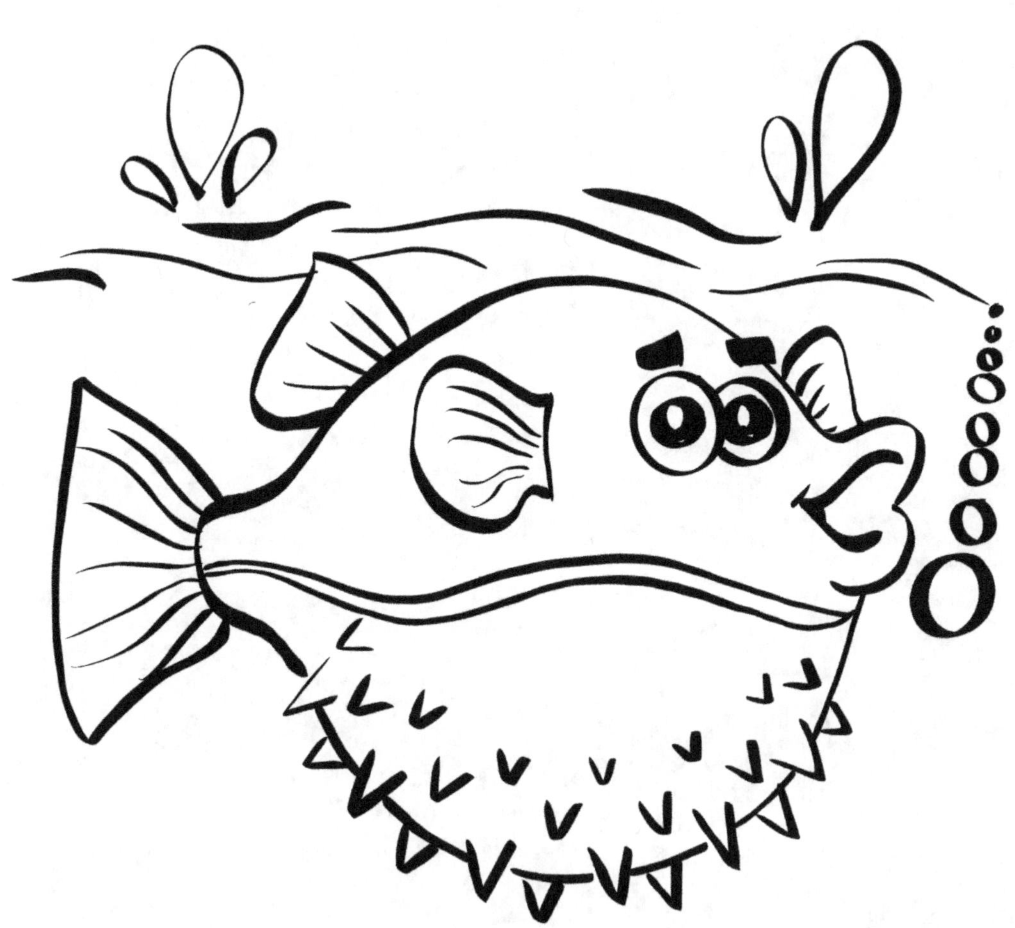

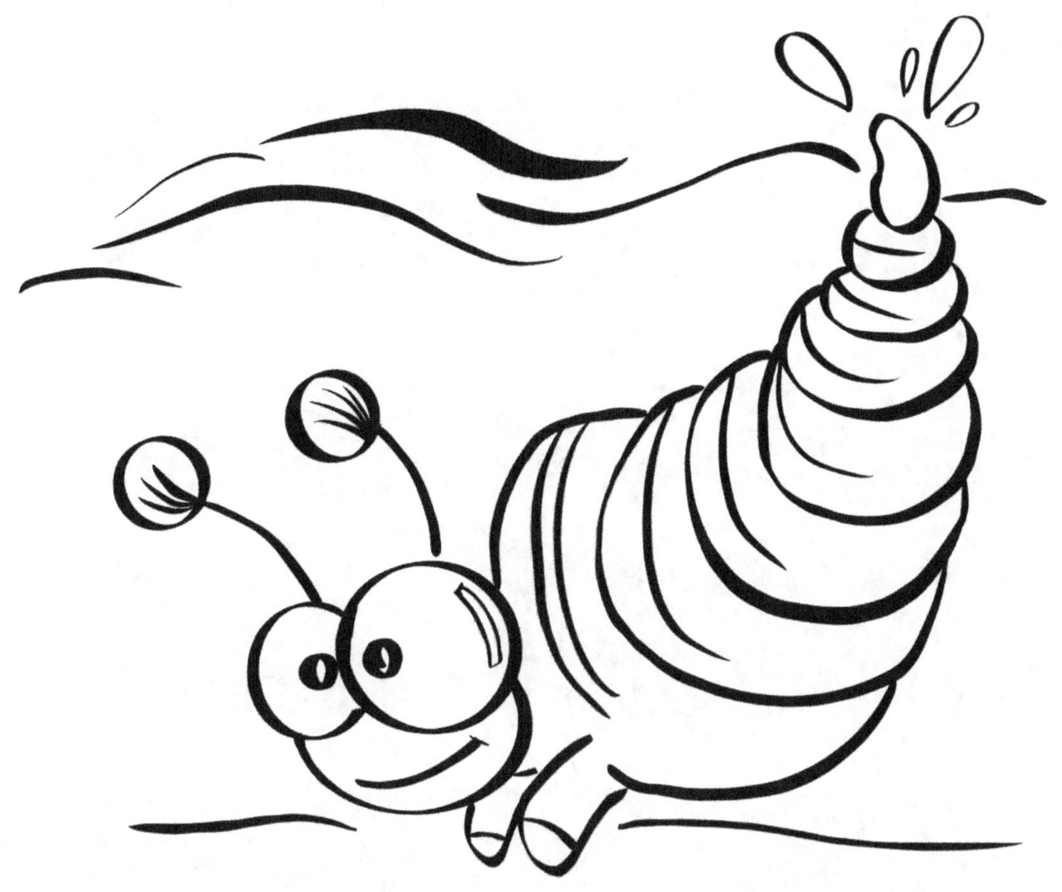